25 Tips
You Didn't
Learn in
School

Destination
REAL
WORLD
SUCCESS AFTER GRADUATION

Amanda K. Haddaway

After more than a decade in the human resources field, including work as a college recruiter, I kept seeing the same things over and over again with our recent high school and college graduates. Our new hires were bright in their subject matter fields, but they were often missing some critical life skills, or soft skills, that are necessary to be successful over the long haul.

It occurred to me that many of these skills aren't being taught in the classroom. In fact, many of us learned these skills in the "school of hard knocks." Rather than expecting these young professionals to know everything as they enter the workforce, I decided to write this guidebook, with the input of several other business professionals, to equip them with the skills necessary to be successful.

Destination Real World: Success after Graduation provides 25 tips to help new college graduates navigate through the challenges of finding and keeping their first jobs and living on their own.

Amanda K. Haddaway
2011

ACKNOWLEDGEMENTS

To my wonderful husband, John: thank you for embracing all my crazy ideas (including writing this book) and loving me in spite of them.

To all four of my parents: Carolyn Perrygo, Dave Folcomer, John Perrygo and Ann Folcomer. Thank you for teaching me to work hard and believe in myself.

A special thank you to my mom, Carolyn Perrygo, for being the best editor around. The dangling participles and excessive exclamation points were no match for your pen.

Thank you to the amazing contributors who made writing the rest of the content an easy process. Your sections added tremendous value to the finished product and I can't thank you enough for your participation in this project.

A portion of the proceeds from this book will be donated to the Maryland Sheriffs' Youth Ranch. MSYR is a 24-hour foster care facility for boys between the ages of 10 and 18. The Ranch's mission is to assist youth in becoming productive members of society. To learn more about the Maryland Sheriffs' Youth Ranch or to make your own tax-deductible donation, please visit *www.msyr.org* or on Facebook at *http://www.facebook.com/Maryland.Sheriffs.Youth.Ranch.*

Designed by

csizmedia, Creative Design Solutions
julicsiz@hotmail.com

TABLE OF CONTENTS

SECTION 1
Finding (and Keeping) a Job

SECTION 2
Making the Transition from School to Work

SECTION 3
Technology and Networking

LEAVING SCHOOL BEHIND: NOW WHAT?

You've probably spent the majority of your life in school and under your parents' (or guardians') watch. Now that you're about to graduate or have recently graduated, there's a whole world waiting for you to discover.

Understandably, this is both an exciting and scary time. There is a certain amount of pressure and stress that comes with deciding on a career path and finding a full-time job. There's also a steep learning curve to quickly obtain some skills that typically aren't learned in the classroom, but are necessary to being successful in the "real world."

No matter what career you end up choosing, some life skills transcend all fields. The ability to work hard and be professional will never go out of style.

Graduation signifies new beginnings, but how do you prepare for all these exciting first steps? It's easier than you may think! Let's get started...

SECTION 1

Finding (and Keeping) a Job

IN THIS SECTION:

1. Career Roadmap
2. Writing Your First Résumé
3. Using Social Media for More than Keeping Up with Friends
4. Beating the Interview Jitters
5. Types of Interviews and How to Prepare
6. Managing Employer Expectations

CHAPTER 1

Career Roadmap

Before you are able to look for a job, you must determine what it is you want to do. One of the best ways to do this is to research different career fields and determine what skills are necessary to succeed in that area.

Most campuses offer career services or some sort of career library that has information on various career fields. You can also do your own Internet research by searching on specific job titles or search phrases that relate to types of jobs. For example, a chemistry major may search for "jobs for chemistry majors."

The career services office or a career counselor at your school may be the best place to find out which employers will be visiting campus and how you can meet them. Many employers set-up informational sessions the day before they conduct on-campus interviews to provide additional information about their organizations. Attending this session can give you an added advantage by learning more about the company before an actual interview. You may also have some additional one-on-one time with the recruiters and interviewers if you make the effort to attend the informational session. Often, these sessions are an infomercial for the company and you can learn facts that can be used during your actual interview.

If you've already graduated and are still looking for a job, many career services programs offer recent graduates assistance with their job searches and may allow you to have continued access to the employers on campus.

Keep in mind that your ultimate career goal is most likely not the job that you will obtain at first, so map out a plan about how you will achieve your ultimate goal. This may include identifying additional training, as well as building skills in various areas.

You should also look into joining professional associations for your desired career field. Many of these organizations have student chapters or offer a discounted rate for new professionals. Some professional organizations also maintain their own job postings and only allow access to members.

Informational interviews are another good way to learn about a company or a career field. An informational interview is not for a job, per se, but rather allows you to learn more about a company or a career field. Many times, the professional providing the information can provide you with guidance on how to get into the career field and talk to you about possible job opportunities.

Informational interviews can be requested by contacting the people who conduct on-campus interviews for a particular company or seeking out your own contacts on LinkedIn, or a similar networking website.

Also consider using your professors for contacts and career information. In many cases, professors have contacts in the business world and may be willing to help you network with professionals in your field.

Your network of contacts is probably larger that you may realize. Don't be shy about asking friends, relatives, friends' parents and other people you know for assistance in your job search. You never know who will have a contact already working in your dream job.

QUICK TIP: One of the biggest complaints from employers is that new graduates don't have realistic expectations on salary and job expectations. As you do research on possible career opportunities, try to gain a complete picture of what the job entails (schedule, number of hours per week, day-to-day responsibilities, etc.) and what entry-level salaries are for the geographic area.

CHAPTER 2

Writing Your First Résumé

Writing your first résumé can be a daunting task. You want to ensure that you communicate that you are the best choice for the job, but you can only provide so much information on a résumé. Make sure you write your résumé so that it highlights what is relevant to the employer and the position you are seeking.

There are several key content areas that should be included in your résumé:

- Knowledge, skills and abilities (KSAs) – these can be from previous part-time jobs, internships and volunteer experiences, as well as skills that you've learned in your classes. Identify only KSAs that are relevant to the job for which you are applying. It is likely that you will have various versions of your résumé for different types of jobs.

- Compile a list of your previous experiences with dates of service. This may include previous jobs, internships, volunteer experience and involvement in student organizations, particularly if you held a leadership position.

- Place the most important information at the top of your résumé. This includes how to contact you and the skills that are relevant to the job that you want to obtain.

- Mention classes and projects that are applicable to the job, but don't go overboard. A brief list of four or five items is acceptable, but two pages is overkill.

- It is not necessary to list your high school name or GPA once you graduate from college or are preparing to graduate and can list an expected graduation date. Some people advise including your college GPA if it is over 3.0 (on a 4.0 scale).

- Try to keep your résumé to one page (and no more than two pages this early in your career) and make sure that it is free from errors. Ask a professor or career services counselor to proofread and provide you with feedback. The more reviews, the better!

- If you are applying for a position in the arts or a creative field, it's acceptable to have a graphically enhanced résumé. However, keep in mind that many employers use software to scan résumés into a database. Most of these software products can't read graphics, so you should also have a Word or text version of your résumé.

ASK THE EXPERT: OVERCOMING SKILL GAPS

By Ed DeLise

One of the major gaps that employers note between their needs and what recent college grads bring to the table is communication skills. The method of communication prevalent and acceptable among teens and college students is not directly transferrable to the business world. Specifically, texting, spelling and grammar errors, and informality are creating wedges that result in missed job opportunities.

Students using email with "texting grammar" are getting shut out of opportunities out of the gate. Employers have to use all correspondence with job candidates, including phone, email and face-to-face conversations, as a basis to project what future conversations will be like both internally and with their clients, should the candidate be hired. Employees have to use great care when communicating with their clients, ensuring that the image, tone and message content represent the company sufficiently. Text messages between friends are a hugely effective and acceptable way to communicate informally, but they are vastly different from business email communication. In formal settings, which include each piece of job correspondence from candidates, more care and diligence must be taken. Students who don't realize the need to communicate in complete, well-structured sentences shut themselves out of potential opportunities.

In the same vein, when job candidates make grammatical and spelling errors in their correspondence, it leaves employers no choice but to exclude them from potential positions. If the candidates don't take the time to ensure that everything is correct when corresponding for something as sensitive as a job opportunity, it comes across as:

- A lack of respect for the firm, the individual they are corresponding with and the position

- Poor judgment

- An inability to potentially represent the company sufficiently to its clients

- A lack of detail orientation or laziness

In school, if you have a few errors on any given paper, you might have a few points deducted from your grade, so the penalty is relatively minimal. In the real world, those same errors will result in much harsher results, including shutting the doors on job opportunities. Employers will assume errors or details missing from résumés and cover letters will correlate with details being left out of correspondence to clients, vendors, business partners and co-workers, which could snowball into larger, costly issues. It is also a poor reflection on the hiring manager's judgment when someone they chose to bring into the firm is incapable of clear communication.

Lastly, formality during the hiring process is something that is currently lacking with job candidates. Although corporate cultures have relaxed from what they were in the past – ties are worn much less frequently, supervisors are called by their first names and spending time socially with co-workers and supervisors can be more common – the hiring process is no place to let your guard down and become too familiar. Showing the proper level of formality shows good judgment and an ability to assess the situation and react accordingly. Candidates who show up wearing sunglasses, and don't remove them during the interview (true story), or who under-dress simply eliminate any chance they had of getting hired, even though they may be perfectly qualified to perform the job requirements otherwise. Keen competition for jobs all too often means that these communication differentiators significantly influence the outcome of the hiring process.

CHAPTER 3

Using Social Media for More Than Keeping Up with Friends

Social media tools, like Facebook, Twitter and LinkedIn, can be valuable resources in not only networking with people you already know, but also with expanding your network to others. The old adage about it's not what you know, but who you know is alive and well in the world of work, so use social media and your connections creatively to find and secure a job.

Social media, though, also has dangers for the young professional. For some, a personal page on a social media site, a blog or a website may include information that isn't necessarily appropriate for the workplace. Before interviewing, go through and analyze your online presence to determine whether a manager or recruiter would be accepting of the comments and images that you have posted. If it doesn't pass the "gut check," then it's best to remove that content.

You may think about searching for your name (and variations of it) on Google to ensure that everything online reflects favorably upon the image you are trying to project to prospective employers. If you find content that you're not particularly proud of, develop a plan to mitigate the problems this content may cause. For example, you may ask the person who posted the objectionable content to remove it because you are searching for a job. If that doesn't work, figure out how you will explain this content should a prospective employer uncover it. Some employers run these same Google searches as a part of their due diligence in the hiring process, so don't be surprised if you are asked. It's best to be proactive and prepared for such a situation.

ASK THE EXPERT: SOCIAL MEDIA AND YOUR JOB SEARCH

By Shannon Smedstad

Some experts say that workers today will spend an average of four years in any given job. Just four years! That means over the course of a typical 30-year career, you could expect to work for more than seven different employers. One skill worth learning now is how to effectively job search.

When your parents searched for their first job, chances are they scanned the local newspaper and mailed in résumés (actually, that's how I conducted my first job search back in the late 90s.). Technology and the times have changed. Today's job seekers have to be savvy on paper, in person and online.

Social media is one of the simplest ways to find jobs, research companies, hear from real employees, get answers and connect with industry representatives. It shouldn't replace traditional job search activities, such as utilizing job boards or your school's career center. Social media should complement your overall strategy.

TIP 1: PROTECT YOUR PERSONAL BRAND

If you decide to use social media in your job search (and you should strongly consider this), you'll want to start by cleaning up your online presence. Make sure your online personal brand represents your professional image. For some of you, this will mean:

- Updating your profile picture

- Asking friends not to tag you in photos

- Removing status updates that use inappropriate language

- Unfriending certain individuals

- Creating a LinkedIn profile

- Increasing your privacy settings

- Making your accounts private versus public, and/or

- Deleting unwanted or inactive accounts

It's no secret that some employers may use social media as a means to conduct background checks and make employment decisions. Don't let a hiring manager find a reason not to consider you for that dream job.

TIP 2: START BUILDING YOUR CONNECTIONS*

Believe it or not, there are many resources and people online that can actually help you in your job search. Finding and building these social connections is easier than you may think.

- **College connections**: Chances are your college career center is already posting jobs on Facebook and creating employer lists on Twitter. Student organizations are tweeting opportunities to members. Your alumni association is posting job discussions via a LinkedIn group. These are all opportunities of which you can take advantage, so connect with your alma mater and tap into your collegiate network.

- **Company connections:** Social media is a great place to find company information. You can watch videos on corporate YouTube channels, listen to podcasts on iTunes or JobsinPods, see photos from company events on Flickr, and interact with company reps on Twitter. Write a list of your top 20 companies, then consider "liking" their corporate career pages, following executives and even @messaging a recruiter.

- **Job connections:** In many cases, social media is a free or low cost means for companies to announce job openings. Many LinkedIn groups offer job discussion boards where real people post jobs. Facebook's Marketplace and company pages often include job postings. On Twitter, you can easily find leads by searching for #jobs, #entrylevel, #hiring or using specific hashtags like #businessmajors, #ITjobs, #YourCity, #jobadvice or #CompanyName.

- **Advice connections:** There are passionate people providing online career advice and getting jobs in front of college grads and alumni. Check out the social media presence for sites such as Careerealism, AfterCollege, New Grad Life, CollegeRecruiter, BrazenCareerist, Experience.com (and the list goes on...). Consider reaching out to your own social network for advice by posing a question to friends and family as this will often solicit additional guidance.

TIP 3: JOIN THE CONVERSATIONS

You can choose to listen in on conversations or you can join them, though putting yourself out there can be a bit scary for some people. Try starting small: post a job- or industry-related question to a LinkedIn group. Consider following a Twitter chat (for example, #hfchat via #HireFriday) and tweet your LinkedIn profile. Or, ask a question on a company's Facebook page. When someone responds, say thank you and maybe send a request to connect.

When engaging your network, remember to be yourself, be polite and be transparent. Remember, it's not all about you. Being engaged online is not a one-way street. Real connections and conversations are happening every day. Reciprocation is appreciated.

TIP 4: CONGRATULATIONS, YOU'RE ALMOST GAINFULLY EMPLOYED

So, you've cleaned up your online presence to represent your grown-up, professional self. You have connected, liked and followed companies, recruiters and career advice gurus. And, you've engaged your network with scintillating career-related conversations. The job offers should start rolling in, right? Not exactly.

Social media connections don't replace the job application or inter-view process. You will still have to fill out online applications and go through standard hiring processes. You'll still need to write an effective résumé, dress to impress and be prepared for in-person interviews. Once a company is lucky enough to hire you, make sure you know their social media policy for employees. Just because you land a job, doesn't necessarily mean you can start tweeting whatever about whomever, whenever.

A little disclaimer from Shannon: The resources and sites listed throughout this section are for informational purposes only, and do not necessarily constitute an endorsement from me. Following the advice provided within this section does not guarantee that you'll find a job, get an interview or receive a job offer. It's up to you to develop and execute a social media job strategy that works for you.

CHAPTER 4
Beating the Interview Jitters

It is totally normal, and expected, to be a little nervous as you go into a job interview. The best way to handle these nerves is to be prepared. Before you arrive at an interview, do your homework!

Quite frankly, first impressions count, so you'll want to ensure that you're putting your best foot forward as soon as you walk into the interview room. You can do this by completing pre-interview homework.

Most companies have an online presence, so it should be relatively easy for you to learn about the company. You should also familiarize yourself with the position for which you are interviewing. If possible, print out a copy of the position description and take it with you to the interview.

Other items that might be worth researching include:

- **Background of the company** – how long has it been in business, how has the company changed over time, what type of work does it do, where are its offices located, who owns the company or is it publicly traded, what type of people does it hire?

- **Position description** – what are the knowledge, skills and abilities required for this position, how do your skills match this position, where is the position located, what will be required of you on a daily basis, is there room for growth?

- **Corporate culture** – this could include items like dress code, work hours, amount of travel required, etc.

CHAPTER 5
Types of Interviews and How to Prepare

One of the best ways to prepare for an interview is to practice. There may be opportunities through career services to participate in mock interviews. A mock interview is usually conducted by an employer, a career services professional or a professor. Essentially, you will be interviewing for a pretend job. Mock interviews are helpful because they can relieve you of nervousness and the interviewers usually are able to provide some feedback on your interview skills.

Maintain eye contact with the interviewers and use non-verbal cues to acknowledge that you are listening to them. You don't want to get into a staring contest with the interviewer, but be alert and active in the dialogue. It's perfectly acceptable to formulate your thoughts before answering an interview question. A brief pause before speaking is normal, so don't be put off by short silent periods. Interviewers may pause briefly to take notes during the interview. This is also common and shouldn't put you on edge.

Many companies utilize behavioral interview techniques. Behavioral interviewing requires the job candidate to provide a situation and then describe the task that comprised the situation, the actions that were taken and the result or outcome.

Questions may be posed to you in a format of "tell me about a time when..." or "give me an example of a time when..." This allows you to share previous work (paid or volunteer) or classroom experiences and the interviewer is able to ascertain what you learned from the experience. Many companies prefer to use this interviewing technique because it provides information on a candidate that isn't likely to be included on a résumé.

At the completion of the interview, it is common for the interviewer to ask you if you have any additional questions. Have a few questions prepared in advance. They can be general questions about the work environment and the type of work that the company does or they can be specific to the position for which you are interviewing. Having something prepared is much better than trying to come up with something under pressure and stumbling in front of the interviewer.

Some interviews may include more than one interviewer. If you are a part of a panel interview, speak to all of the interviewers by looking at them while you respond. When the interview concludes, thank each person for their time and close with a firm handshake. It's also appropriate to ask for their business cards so that you can send a follow-up thank you note or email after the interview.

CHAPTER 6

Managing Employer Expectations

Your employer has hired you to do a job and that is precisely what you must do while at work. Managers appreciate employees who are focused on their tasks and perform to the best of their abilities. Other ways to impress your employer include:

- Showing up on time, or even early. It's very difficult to do your job effectively if you are not present.

- Asking questions for clarity and better understanding. You're not expected to know everything. By asking specific and relevant questions, your employer will know that you are engaged in the process of completing the project at hand.

- Listen! We have two ears and one mouth for a reason, so listen twice as much as you speak.

Check in with your manager on a regular basis. Most companies only do formal performance reviews at the six-month or yearly anniversary mark, but it's important to monitor your progress along the way. Ask your manager for five or ten minutes monthly to discuss what you're doing well and what you could do better. Take that feedback and act upon it.

QUICK TIP: Just like your personal appearance, the appearance of your workspace—whether a desk, cubicle or office—should not look like a messy dorm room or high school locker. Reflecting your best professional self in your personal and work space appearance builds credibility and advances your career.

ASK THE EXPERT: GAME PLAN FOR A STELLAR ROOKIE SEASON

By Kristy Jackson

Let's face it: starting a new job kind of feels like being a freshman all over again. After the status and security that comes from being a senior, suddenly becoming the new kid on the team just isn't that fun. Use these simple tips to help you ace your rookie season at your new job:

1. PRACTICE THE FUNDAMENTALS

Are you spending your days working on less than intriguing projects? It can be disheartening when your first job doesn't meet your expectations. Maybe you feel like the work you're doing doesn't matter or that the projects you are assigned are beneath your skill set. But, sometimes there is a bigger picture than you realize. Perhaps there is a reason why your boss is having you work on a particular project. Similarly, remember, your rookie year is kind of a proving ground. Even if you were a star in school, your new boss and colleagues may still see you as a kid. It's up to you to prove that you can handle the new responsibilities.

How to shine? Quickly master your tasks. Once you demonstrate your ability to handle the basics, you should soon be assigned to more challenging work. In the meantime, do you know how your work contributes to the good of the team? Figure that out, and you'll soon discover ways to contribute more. And most importantly, make sure your boss and colleagues see you acting like an adult. In other words, call if you're sick, keep workplace conversations on safe topics, meet your deadlines, introduce yourself to others, dress a step better than you have to, and always use spell check on your messages. Attitude and effort can propel you a long way.

2. LEARN THE TEAM

Switching suddenly from academia to the workplace might bring a bit of culture shock. After spending four (or more) years on a campus filled primarily with young people, it can be quite startling to hear break room conversations about diapers, mortgages and grandkids. It's no wonder if you feel like you don't fit in quite anywhere. And, while you might have one boss, you may have a variety of team leaders and unofficial supervisors observing your work. It can be hard to tell who really matters.

How to shine? If you're feeling lonely or invisible on the job, the best thing you can do is break out of your comfort zone and introduce yourself to people. Reach out. And don't just schmooze with the bosses—make sure you know the names of secretaries, assistants, security guards and the IT people. Try to look past the age issue: the 30-year old in the next cubicle could end up being your next boss and the 60-year old secretary just might become your biggest ally. If your organization has committees, consider joining one. It's a smart way to meet people and raise your profile at the same time. Finally, if you are new to your community, see if the city has a young professionals' network designed to help you connect with other young people. It could save your sanity.

3. STUDY THE COMPETITION

One of the best ways to elevate yourself is to learn more about what's happening in your industry. If you're in business, who are your company's main competitors? If you work for a nonprofit, are you aware of organizations that have missions similar to yours who are competing for the same funding? Ideally, you would have started this process in college while you were taking senior-level classes and preparing for your interviews. Did your professors introduce you to any professional groups or assign readings from their journals? Those are excellent resources for figuring out the key players in your industry.

How to shine? Ask your colleagues if there are industry publications that they read. And then read them. After that, see if you can tag along with them for one of their next networking meetings. This kind of involvement will help you to really understand how your work fits in with the bigger picture. Likewise, ask your boss to put you on the distribution lists for any journals or professional publications that your office receives. Be sure to comment on articles after you've read them, so that your boss knows of your interest and desire to learn. Finally, if you have a chance to attend a conference, take it. Participate in as many workshops as you can. You might be pleasantly surprised at how many great ideas you gather that could just as easily be implemented in your organization.

4. GET A GAME PLAN

The art of being independent and self-directed might be one of your biggest challenges. In school, you probably had advisors and faculty who were there every step of the way to make sure you did your best work and met all of your deadlines. The workplace isn't like that. You'll probably be surprised at how much freedom you have on a daily basis. As long as your work is being finished, you probably won't hear a whole lot from your boss. Plus, there won't be any hand-holding to help you figure out how to climb to the next rung. Your boss hired you to do a job. As hard as it may be to hear, it's not likely that your boss is going to make it a priority to advance your career.

How to shine? Make the most of your first year at your job. Once you tackle the routine tasks, make it a priority to talk with your boss or other mentor about what else you can do to contribute and grow. Are there new assignments you could tackle? Training sessions you could attend? Meetings you could observe? Or, if you are intrigued with another department, look into collaborative ventures. Even if you don't see yourself staying with this organization for the long term, you'll want to walk away with a stellar reputation, a strong recommendation and an enhanced professional network, so make your time count. Remember, you get what you go for, so take all that you can from the experience.

TIPS FOR PARENTS: Resist the temptation to act like your child's agent! Trust me: it's not your place to try discussing your child's employment issues with his or her new boss. Think of your role as "strength training coach"—you are there to help your child develop skills and to find resources, but not for the main event. If your child needs more money, more vacation time or more interesting work, it's up to your young adult child to ask for it.

Making the Transition from School to Work

IN THIS SECTION:

CHAPTER 7

Finding a Place to Live

One of the biggest initial decisions that you will make is about where you will live. Many students find that going back home is the most affordable and perhaps only option until some money can be saved up to go out on their own. If you're able to find your own housing, make sure you have a budget.

Figure out how much money you'll have coming in with each paycheck (after taxes and other deductions) and how much you'll need to spend on other expenses. Most companies spell out how much you will be paid in a formal offer letter. If this information is unclear, make sure you ask your recruiter or contact at the company for some additional details.

The offer letter will have your salary or hourly wages listed before taxes are taken out. This is an important distinction, as you'll quickly learn that a good percentage of your earnings go to the government for state and federal taxes and Medicare. Additionally, your employer may make pre-tax deductions from your paycheck to cover health insurance premiums and 401(k) or retirement plan contributions.

If you're taking a position that pays commission, find out if you'll be able to take a weekly or monthly draw and make sure you understand how this system works if you don't make sales goals during your first few weeks or months.

You'll also need to find out how frequently you will be paid. Companies vary in the ways that they pay their employees. Some pay weekly, while others pay bi-weekly or twice a month. Commissions are often only paid one time per month. This information will be important to you as you build your weekly and monthly budgets.

CHAPTER 8
Living Alone or Finding a Roommate?

If you lived away from home during college, you may already be familiar with having a roommate. If you can tolerate it, having a roommate or two can dramatically help in cutting initial housing costs. It's best to select roommates who have similar ambitions and career goals. It can be a recipe for disaster if you move in with someone who likes to have parties all night and you have to be at work at 7 a.m.

Living with someone else is a serious commitment, so make sure you ask your prospective roommates plenty of questions before signing a lease. Landlords and property management companies don't have to let you out of a lease if your roommates don't work out. Save yourself an expensive consequence and a lot of headaches and frustration by doing your homework before agreeing to move in with someone.

You should consider your own personal habits which may be annoying to other people, as well as asking questions about your prospective roommate's cleanliness, noise, work schedule, thoughts on having parties and guests over during the work week and any other topic that you feel needs to be discussed.

QUICK TIP: Just because you know someone doesn't mean you know how he or she lives. Ask plenty of questions upfront to eliminate future problems. Your home should be a place in which you want to spend time, but a problematic roommate can create lots of unwanted and unneeded stress.

CHAPTER 9
What to Expect When Renting

If you decide to rent, you will most likely have to pay for some or all of your utilities. This may include electric, gas, water, cable/satellite TV, internet, trash pick-up, etc. Depending on where you live, you may also have community association or condo fees on top of your monthly rent.

Renters' insurance is required by some property management companies and it is a good idea to protect your belongings even if it's not required by your lease, so figure in that cost to your monthly budget, too. Most insurance brokers can provide you with a quote based on the address of your new home. You'll need to provide the broker with the value of your belongings (an estimate is acceptable) and if you have any extremely valuable items. The valuable items may require additional insurance coverage in case of loss or damage.

If you're not sure where to start, ask your family members who they use for homeowner's or renter's insurance. Another possibility is to ask your auto insurance carrier if their company offers renter's insurance. In some cases, you may be eligible for a small discount if you have your auto and renter's insurance through the same company.

Most property management companies require you to sign a lease agreement. Make sure you read all of the fine print. The lease agreement is a binding contract. It may include clauses that require you to pay additional fees if you terminate your lease early, cause property damage or be fined for a variety of other mishaps. If this is your first lease, you may want to have a more experienced renter review it to make sure that the language is standard.

Don't be surprised if the landlord or management company requires a security deposit or an amount of money equal to one or two months' rent as an "insurance policy" in case damage occurs while you live there.

Before you take possession of the actual property, schedule a walk-through with the landlord or property manager to test out the plumbing, electrical and other features, as well as document any visible damage. You may consider taking a digital camera along with you that has a date stamp on the photos in case existing damage comes into question when you decide to vacate the property at the end of the lease.

Be leery of landlords who aren't willing to do a walk-through of the actual property that you are renting or refuse to sign a lease agreement. As a renter or tenant, you have rights to fair housing standards. Most states have minimum guidelines to which a landlord must adhere. For example, many states require running water and properly functioning heat. It may be shocking to think about these things not working, but there are plenty of rental properties across the country in disrepair.

CHAPTER 10
Living Expenses

Your rent payment will most likely be the largest expense that you have each month. In addition to rent, other monthly expenses include gas for your vehicle, groceries/food expenses, car payments, car insurance and incidentals. Many students also leave school with the burden of hefty student loans. In most cases, these loans need to be repaid starting soon after your education is complete. Make sure that you understand the terms of the loan and the repayment schedule. A student loan is very similar to a mortgage in that your failure to pay on time can adversely impact your credit score for many years going forward. Defaulting on a student loan is a terrible idea, so be sure to take your repayment responsibilities seriously.

If possible, try to save a little each paycheck in case something unexpected comes up. As you advance in your career, many financial advisors recommend having six-month's salary in your savings account. This is hard to imagine when you're first starting out, but you'll be amazed at how quickly you can build a "rainy day" fund by just saving $20 or $50 per paycheck or per month.

Retirement may seem VERY far away, but try to put a little money into your 401(k) or another retirement fund. People who start saving in their early 20's are much better off than those who wait until age 30 or later. If your employer offers a dollar-for-dollar match, try to take advantage of that "free money." Your company's human resources department should be able to explain what benefits are available and how you can maximize your retirement savings.

When you're planning for your initial housing expenses, also consider if you'll need to purchase furniture. Check with friends and family members to see if they have any items that they would be willing to donate. If not, try to find used items and items on sale to help reduce your costs. If you plan on cooking, you'll also need to obtain a basic set of pots and pans, dishes, flatware and cooking utensils.

You will also need linens and towels for your bedroom and bathroom. Again, check with friends and family members for any hand-me-downs. Most major retailers put these items on sale monthly and around holidays. Discount retailers like Marshalls and T.J.Maxx are also good places to purchase towels and sheets.

It's not much fun to live paycheck to paycheck, so try to find accommodations that will fit within your means. That is, try to ensure that your rent and expenses still leave a little money left over for incidentals and social events.

QUICK TIP: Since this will be one of your first opportunities to start building your credit history, make sure you take the responsibilities of setting up a household seriously. Be mindful of due dates for utility bills and rent and make sure that you pay them on time. Many banks offer online bill payment that allows you to set-up bill payment reminders and schedule recurring payments (bills that are the same amount every month).

CHAPTER 11

What You Do Now Stays with You for a Long Time

Many companies require background checks for new employees. The complexity and thoroughness of the search is dependent on the type of career field you are entering and the company's policy. It is important to understand that most background checks go back at least seven years. Positions requiring top-level security clearances may go back even further. Everything from traffic violations to more serious offenses could show up on your background report. If an employer asks you in advance of conducting the report if you've ever been arrested or in any sort of legal trouble, it is always best to tell the truth. It will be at the employer's discretion as to whether this is a "deal breaker" for hiring you. However, it is much worse to not disclose this information and then have the company find out that you lied. As is the case with most things in life, honesty is the best policy.

It is also important to note that your first job might not be your dream job, or even the career that you think you want. As you interview for future jobs, you will need to disclose previous employment on your résumé and job applications. If you give your best effort at every job, it is less likely that you will receive a bad reference check if a prospective employer checks into your previous employment.

Work is called work for a reason. It's not always fun, but try to give your best effort every day and have a positive attitude. It makes a big difference as you move forward in your career.

CHAPTER 12

Professionalism and Maturity

One of the biggest stumbling blocks that young professionals encounter is knowing how to act in the world of work. There are marked differences between school and work and many of these organizational differences are not taught in a classroom.

Each company has its own norms and accepted behaviors. As a new employee, you will need to observe and try to absorb what is and isn't acceptable. Try to do your homework by reading things like the employee handbook and any information that the company sends to you prior to your start date. It is advisable to also look at the company's website and try to research the company to the best of your ability.

If you're unclear on something, ask your recruiter or your hiring manager. Make sure you understand the dress code and when and where you are expected to report on your first day of employment.

If the dress code is business casual, make sure you clarify what is and isn't appropriate. Business casual has become the norm for many employers, but many people are still unclear on what this means. For some, it means khakis and polo shirts, casual pants, casual dresses, etc. Some companies have a business casual policy that excludes jeans or open-toed shoes. The term is very subjective, so look around the workplace when you visit to observe what others are wearing and try to find the company's definition in its employee handbook.

Some companies have one dress code when you're working in the office and another when you're meeting with clients. The generally accepted rule is to dress like the client or one step above, but double-check with your supervisor.

QUICK TIP: One of my first managers always told me to "dress for the job you want." This is good advice and has been helpful throughout my career. If you're dressing like your manager or the people in the next hierarchical level of the company, you are probably appropriate for the workplace.

CHAPTER 13

The Power of Please and Thank You—Three Simple, Yet Very Important Words

When we were children, "please" and "thank you" were referred to as "magic words" that were to be used when we were asking for something and then, in turn, receiving something. Although we've all outgrown the reminders from our parents, these words have certainly not lost their enchantment. In fact, these words are so important that almost every language has some equivalent with similar meaning.

Please and thank you still have a prominent place in the business world and young professionals should use them at every opportunity.

By using common courtesies, you demonstrate that you respect the people with whom you are dealing. Even if you don't work in a customer service job, keep an attitude of customer service. Your colleagues and, more importantly, your superiors will begin to realize that you are a go-to person if you're almost always pleasant.

There are several other free and very easy gestures that go a long way in life. Consider doing the following on a daily basis:

- Hold the door for people who are entering or exiting a building behind you.

- Wait your turn in line and don't complain when it's a lengthy wait.

- Apologize if you have erred – everyone makes mistakes occasionally. Accept your mistake and learn from it.

- Say excuse me when you inadvertently bump into someone else.

These very basic actions go a long way in starting your career off right.

ASK THE EXPERT: THE BEST OF EVERYTHING

By Constance Dunn

When you actively and consistently engage the traditional rules of correct behavior some may look at you like you are a Martian. That is because these days civility, manners, courtesy, etiquette – however you refer to positive social behavior – appear to be at an all-time low. This means that great big displays of positive social behavior are needed now more than ever.

A person displaying a lot of regard for others is a good thing. Few people doing so is most certainly not and results in a society where the terrible things that you read and hear about each day happen with even greater frequency.

Social behavior, both good and bad, is contagious. It is also personal. It is your most basic mode of communicating with others. You reveal to others who you are, where you are from, what you think about yourself and them by the way you behave.

The ability to display positive social behavior has zip, zero, nothing to do with economics or ZIP codes or having a dashing face or figure. You've probably known more than one person with a Midas bank account or cover model looks who lives in the swankiest part of town and behaves like the worst sort of gnome imaginable. Conversely you've no doubt experienced a place or person as humble and plain as they come, yet brimming with warmth, dignity and elegance. Just being there made you want to stand up straighter, speak with more clarity and substance and be your best in thought, speech and manner.

When you treat yourself and others with dignity and respect, what exactly does it get you? The best of everything.

When you present your best self to the world you become the person that everyone wants to be around. There is something about being the most decent girl or guy in the room that is not just magnetic, but contagious, and everyone wants what you've got.

Positive social behavior attracts those who enjoy being in the company of other positive, polished and respectful people, and does a lovely job of warding off those gnomes of which we spoke earlier. This has something to do with the *contrast principle*, which highlights the fact that gnomes, when placed next to class acts like you, look like mega-gnomes and class acts look even classier.

A bona fide lady or gentleman enjoys the frequent advantage of being recognized as such by those in positions to say "yes" to their professional aspirations. Those job interviews that take place over lunch or dinner exist for one reason: your potential employers want to see how you act in the real world.

And on the friend and romance front: ever notice that decent men and women tend to gravitate towards, hang out with, date and marry other decent folks?

It might also be a good time to mention that displaying positive social behavior is *free*. As in, it costs you nothing, but gets you everything. And you are not the sole beneficiary of its riches because you make any place better simply by walking in the front door. The addition of decency, empathy, elegance and warmth to a room, any room, is always a big plus.

Positive social behavior is not off-limits to anyone. You may have been born and raised in one of the nine circles of hell and have the scars to prove it. (And I am sorry for that, by the way.) However, here's the good news: you own a lovely and thief-proof thing called *free will*. Use it to not emulate the actions of those around you whom you don't respect or want to be like. Be *you* at your best even when it's not what the "cool kids" are doing.

It might mean that you need to learn from scratch or seriously brush up on your table manners or introductions or grooming or business etiquette. Cultivate your capabilities in these things; read about them and do them over and over again until they seem like part of you, and soon enough they will be.

You are the sole author of your behavior. You are also its guardian. This means that you must remain diligent about maintaining the quality of it, no matter in what circumstances you find yourself. In other words, don't cave. Don't cave when you are around those gnomes who, incidentally, like to hang around with other gnomes and delight in bringing down winners and declassing class acts. Don't cave out of some desire to relate to others or please someone to fit in or stand out.

Remember, standards are lowered with remarkable speed and are not nearly as easy to pull up as they are to pull down.

You, the lady. You, the gentleman. *You at your best* will reap some heady rewards in this life, from the way you feel about yourself to the quality of your mate, job, friends and even the way you're treated when you walk in a door.

In an age of diminishing civility, there is great public demand for your supply of positive social behavior. It has the remarkable power to get you the best of everything, so for the benefit of your life engage in big public displays of positive social behavior wherever you go. I, for one, am looking forward to seeing them.

CHAPTER 14

Grooming and Appearance— What is and isn't Appropriate in the Workplace

This topic was briefly mentioned in an earlier chapter, but it's a topic that deserves more attention. Proper grooming and ensuring that your appearance is workplace-appropriate can set you apart from the competition.

Each company has its own dress code, but there are some things that apply to all types of dress codes:

- Make sure your clothes are clean and in good repair. Nothing says unprofessional like a shirt with stains and pants with holes in them. Have a set of clothes for work and a set of clothes for hanging out, but don't wear the latter set to work.

- Invest in an iron and find a good dry cleaner. Certain articles of clothing require pressing or care by a dry cleaner. Pants generally look better when they have been professionally pressed. Dry cleaning costs can be expensive, so try to find coupons or use a dry cleaner that offers a discount on certain days of the week or volume discounts for multiple pieces of clothing. Also, some pants can be worn a few times without sending them back to the cleaners each time if you hang them up as soon as you're finished wearing them.

- Dress conservatively. It's hard to err on the side of modest dressing.

A QUICK NOTE ON TATTOOS AND BODY PIERCINGS

In recent years, the number of people with tattoos and body piercings has increased. These artistic forms of self-expression may not be welcome in some workplaces. Don't be surprised if you are asked to remove body piercings while in the office or cover tattoos with clothing.

Each employer has a different policy, so make sure you understand what is allowed in your prospective workplace. As mentioned earlier, it's always best to err on the side of being overly conservative in your appearance.

Employers may also have a preference for "natural" hair colors. To clarify, purple is not a natural hair color and may be frowned upon by some companies.

If you really want a particular job, you might consider removing your piercings and covering your tattoos before the interview. If you feel strongly about your body art, make sure you find a workplace that's accepting of your piercings and/or tattoos.

CHAPTER 15

The Importance of Punctuality and Being Present

During college, you may have missed a few early morning classes and there weren't too many repercussions. The workplace, however, is very different. Most employers expect their employees to be punctual and arrive on time in the morning and work a full day. Repeated tardiness or absences without a good reason can be cause for being fired.

In fact, one of the most common complaints about hiring young professionals is their lack of punctuality. Although many employers don't require that employees punch in on a time clock when they arrive, there is an unwritten expectation that employees should be in the office during working hours. Each workplace is different, but it will see you a long way if you can figure out very early into your career when you are expected to be working.

In many salaried positions (those not eligible for overtime wages), there is an unwritten expectation that employees will work extra hours, as necessary. This doesn't mean that you can't have a life outside of work or that you need to feel chained to your desk, but it does mean that a nine-to-five office job may require you to go in early and stay late for certain projects. This is another area where observing your manager and co-workers can give you hints as to what's expected.

Not only do employers expect you to be there physically, they also expect you to be there mentally. What does this mean? Quite simply, they expect that you will show up, you'll be on task and you'll be engaged in your work. You might have been able to pull off hiding out in the back of a college lecture hall, but at work, you must contribute. So show up and work hard!

CHAPTER 16

Talking the Talk—Why Communication Skills Matter

Communication in the workplace can take many forms, so you'll need to determine what the accepted norms are for your employer. For example, some teams have weekly meetings to check on everyone's progress and chat about any issues that have come up during the prior week. Some teams work remotely and only communicate via email and phone. Whatever type of communication you are using, make sure that you are participating in the discussion, asking questions where necessary and providing responses when asked.

No matter what, make sure that your communication is professional in its tone. What you say is a huge reflection on you, so make sure you think before you speak. No one expects you to know all the answers, so freely admit if you're not sure about something and offer to get back to the person once you have more information.

If you're able to establish credibility early in your career, you will have a much easier time going forward. Tell the truth and be sincere. You will quickly earn your co-workers' and managers' trust if you exhibit these qualities.

In many workplaces and career fields, there is an expectation that you will work with other people on projects during the course of your employment. It's sometimes tough to get along with varying personalities and that is precisely why clear communication is so important. Take time to listen to other people's points of view. You may not always agree, but it's likely that you can learn something new by being open to other perspectives.

As a young professional, you will be expected to communicate with co-workers, your manager and possibly more senior leaders within the organization. Many colleges require public speaking courses and a basic introductory communications class to better prepare students for the workplace, but sometimes this isn't quite enough. If you need help finding your voice and speaking in front of others, practice does help. There are also organizations like Toastmasters International that coach professionals in their presentation abilities.

Also remember that a big part of communication is receiving a message. Young professionals need to be open to receiving direction and feedback from co-workers and managers within the organization. Most seasoned professionals can tell you that they have been on the receiving end of criticism at some point in their careers. Listen to the feedback and then take action to improve upon whatever was cited in the discussion as an area for improvement. No one is perfect, so don't expect to know everything. Take initiative to correct the issue going forward and learn from the experience.

CHAPTER 17

When Your Body Does the Talking

The words that come out of your mouth are only one piece of the communication pie. Savvy professionals understand that their bodies also do the "talking." In fact, the way that you carry yourself in the workplace can have a great impact on how people perceive you.

For example, good posture may indicate that you are alert and engaged in the work that you are doing. Slouching, on the other hand, may be perceived as a sign of laziness or a disinterest in the work.

You should also be aware of what you do with your arms when you're speaking. To show that you are open and engaging, consider leaving your arms at your side and not crossed over your chest.

Facial expressions should remain neutral or positive. If you're listening to someone speak, you may want to occasionally nod to indicate that you are listening to their message and absorbing it. Make eye contact with the speaker when possible.

One of the best ways to make sure that your body language is appropriate is to have a friend or family member watch you and see if you do any gestures or movements that could be construed as inappropriate in the workplace. Listen to the feedback and make adjustments as necessary. You might also consider making a video recording of yourself giving a presentation. Many of us project non-verbal cues of which we're not even aware. By watching yourself on video, you can see if there are behaviors that should be changed or altered.

QUICK TIP: If you will be working or traveling internationally, make sure that you are aware of that country's accepted body language norms. In some countries, it is disrespectful to look someone directly in the eye, which is totally counterintuitive to what we do in the United States.

CHAPTER 18
Dealing with Stress as a Young Professional

It's totally normal to feel some stress while making the transition from school to work. After all, you are encountering a lot of life changes and new beginnings.

The important part is making sure that the stress doesn't overtake your life. Your stress can be minimized by doing the following things:

- **Develop a plan.** We already talked about developing a career roadmap in Section 1, but you should consider mapping out a plan for where you're going to live, how you will pay your bills, etc.

- **Talk to your friends and family.** The people who care about you can be valuable resources as sounding boards and as people who can offer you advice. Sometimes it's a stress reducer to just talk about a problem or dilemma you are experiencing. And remember, all of your friends from school are going through very similar experiences so they can probably relate to the way that you're feeling.

- **Don't panic.** Have a positive attitude – this should be an exciting time for you, so don't lose sight of that!

Some people also feel less stressed when they take some time for themselves. This may include working out at the gym, reading a book or doing something else fun. Figure out what works for you and do that activity anytime you feel the weight of the world coming down upon you.

Also, keep everything in perspective. Although your transition from school to work may seem overwhelming, think about all the people who made this transition before you and lived to tell about it … with a smile.

CHAPTER 19

Working Well with Others and Navigating Work Relationships

Building relationships is an important component of being success-ful in the workplace. This doesn't mean that you need to be completely extroverted in every situation, but it does mean that you need to make an effort to get to know the people with whom you work and learn about what skills and abilities they bring to the table.

Although you are at work to do a job, it will be a much more pleasant experience if you enjoy the company of the people on your team or in your department, so try to get off to a good start. The expression about only getting one chance to make a first impression is abso-lutely true, so make sure you put your best foot forward each and every time you encounter a new colleague.

If you're giving your best effort every day, your co-workers will begin to realize that they can depend on you to do a good job. Also, as hard as it may be sometimes, try to have a good attitude at work. No one likes to work with someone who is constantly negative and complains about every little task.

Here are a few additional tips to encourage positive working relationships:

- Be friendly and encouraging to co-workers.

- Be responsible – if you say you're going to do something, do it. If you're unable to complete a task for some reason, make sure that information is communicated to all team members who would be impacted.

- If you share an office, be considerate. Find out how your office mate works and be respectful. For example, some people need to work in complete silence, while others enjoy background music. Make sure that you're not inadvertently making your office mate crazy with your personal habits.

- Understand that people are unique and dwell on their positive qualities, not their negative qualities. It's acceptable to not be friends with everyone, but try to at least be professional and cordial in your interactions.

- Rise above office gossip. No one wants to earn the reputation of being the office busybody.

- Communicate, communicate, communicate! Your co-workers are not mind readers, so make sure that you're communicating with them and your manager on a regular basis.

CHAPTER 20

Wait... I Have to Cook for Myself?

For many recent graduates, preparing meals is one of the toughest adjustments. If you lived at home or in a campus dorm, it's likely that you had someone making your meals for you without much effort other than showing up to the table.

While some larger corporations have in-house cafeterias, it is likely that you will need to prepare at least some meals for yourself. No one is expecting you to concoct restaurant-quality gourmet meals, but you should know the basics.

Since you will need to budget your paycheck to cover all of your newfound expenses, determine how much you can spend on food per month (or per week). This figure should also include any meals that you plan to eat in restaurants.

Once you calculate the total amount, determine how much you can spend per meal. The figure may be pretty small when you start your career and coupons may become your best friends, but you need to know this so that you don't blow your entire month's budget on food.

If you're really averse to cooking, many grocery stores offer pre-made meals that require only heating. One caution: check the nutritional facts, as some of these meals are high in calories, fat and/or sodium.

Once you get into a routine of grocery shopping and see what items you buy frequently, visit various grocery stores in your area to see which ones offer the best prices. You may want to also comparison shop on different quantities of the same item. Sometimes buying an item in bulk is cheaper than buying a single-serve portion.

If you're feeling adventurous with your cooking skills, find recipes online and in cookbooks to build a repertoire of go-to meal plans. Family members are often a good source of recipes for those comfort food classics that remind you of home.

CHAPTER 21

Dining Etiquette and Table Manners

At some point in your career, it is almost certain that you will need to have a meal with your manager or a client. Proper table manners go a long way in showing your dining companion that you are a professional both inside and outside of the workplace.

Make sure that you are dressed appropriately for the restaurant. In some places, a suit jacket and tie are still required for gentlemen. Most restaurants will be happy to share their dress codes if you call them and ask. It's better to ask the question than show up in jeans to a formal dining room.

Napkins should be placed on your lap when you sit down. If you must leave the table, excuse yourself and place the napkin loosely folded on your chair until you return.

Unless you've learned these skills previously, you may be a little uncertain of which fork to use, on which bread plate to place your roll and from which glass to drink. However, with a little practice knowing these simple rules can save you lots of embarrassment at the table.

You'll be amazed at how many people don't have a good command of table etiquette. Mastering these simple guidelines can give you an advantage.

ASK THE EXPERT: A CRASH COURSE IN TABLE MANNERS AND DINING ETIQUETTE

By Qiana Broughton

Etiquette? Table manners? It sounds easy, right? The concept of proper social behavior is older than our founding fathers and yet the significance of etiquette and how people interact during the course of a meal has been diminished along with our daily social interactions.

Regardless of the social climate, manners directly relate to one's social maturity. Needless to say, the first step to addressing a lack of manners is to recognize that table manners are indeed important to your professional well-being.

In fact, etiquette and table manners matter more than you may want to give credit to your parents and teachers. Good manners don't have to be work – a little preparation can go a long way toward making your time enjoyable. Besides, we're talking food here. What's not to love? Enjoy your dinner date, make a good impression on a college professor or during a business lunch. With a little table manner know-how, you'll impress even your harshest critic.

First things first: dress appropriately for the occasion! Formal dinners call for tuxedos and ball gowns. For today's business lunch or dinner, professional business attire will suffice. For men, that means a suit and tie or slacks and a sport coat. Women should stick to office attire such as a blouse with slacks or knee length skirts and dresses. In a professional setting it's best to keep your arms and chest area adequately covered.

Next, a prompt arrival is well appreciated. A formal dinner can be delayed up to 20 minutes as a courtesy for late guests. Restaurant dinners tend to allow less leeway, since reservations are required. Personal items such as coats should be stored in a specified area as outlined by the host or hostess. Purses can be held on the lap or stored on the floor.

Traditionally, cocktails and refreshments are served for approximately 30 minutes, with dinner being announced at least 15 minutes prior to seating. With respect to weddings, the "cocktail" hour usually refers to light refreshments and hors d'oeuvres prior to dinner. However, this is not the case during a formal dinner setting. Hors d'oeuvres are held back to preserve the guests' appetites.

Depending on the formality of the event, guest seating may be specifically marked by place cards or guests may be allowed to choose their own seats in a less formal setting. As a rule of thumb, you don't want to clutter the table setting in any way, so refrain from bringing additional glasses or dinnerware to the dinner table. Men stand until women are seated. A gentleman assists the lady to the right with seating by gently pulling out and pushing in her seat, then seating himself once all ladies are seated.

What's on the menu? Menu cards are usually displayed at each table setting to take away the guesswork of what's for dinner. To make sense of the place setting, use your plate as a center point and use utensils farthest from the plate first, from the outside going inward. Dessert utensils are usually placed horizontally above your plate or, for the less formal dinner, they can be brought out with the dessert. All drinking glasses lie at the top right corner of your table setting, while a small service plate and utensil, usually for bread and butter, lie at the top left corner of the place setting, just above your forks. Still not sure what fork comes first and which knife to use? Think of it this way, you eat with a fork (left), so additional plating will also be on the left. Food is also served on the left. Drinks on the right! Should dinners only include one or two courses, only one or two forks or knives may be arranged on the table. You may want to draw this layout a few times. The idea is to commit the basics to memory in efforts to make your dining experience more enjoyable. Now, spread your napkin in your lap and gear up for a delicious meal!

When eating your dinner, most of the "rules" you've heard are probably true. I can't begin to count the number of times my mother told me to sit up straight, keep my elbows off the table and chew with my mouth closed. Sip; don't slurp. Unpleasant sounds such as belching and smacking are best avoided. You may want to keep portions small and eat at a steady pace. For business dining, you want to keep your food selection simple to avoid unpleasant comments from fellow diners. For soup you want to scoop away from your face. For the main course, etiquette calls that you eat with your utensils, fork in the left hand and knife in the right, facing downward, gently touching the plate in an "X" motion. Specifically, you'll hold the food with your fork, while cutting across the top of the fork prongs, in an "X" motion to gently slice food. Refrain from sawing, as if you're cutting a piece of wood. Sawing food may result in random bites being propelled toward other guests. Cut only enough for each bite. As you're eating, you may rest the utensils in an "X" position across your plate. When you are completely finished with each course, take both utensils into the right hand and rest them gently on the plate.

Finish off dessert and coffee service quietly and remember to keep the conversation light. Refrain from talking about personal affairs, but listen if they are mentioned. Are you comfortable yet? Having good manners and etiquette will come as second nature to you over time. It's a small price to pay when you get the job, get the grade or get the relationship all while having a wonderful dining experience!

CHAPTER 22

Networking for Career Success

ASK THE EXPERT: DO YOU HAVE WHAT IT TAKES TO SCHMOOZE?

By Eileen Schlesier

Some people are born social butterflies. They love nothing more than chatting up strangers on the street or in the supermarket checkout line. For others, the conversations don't come as easy. Whether it is at a formal networking event, a client dinner, a tradeshow or an industry party, opportunities for expanding your network are plentiful and are critical in everyday business. If you are nervous, know that with practice it does get easier. Successful networking is a skill that grows every time you exercise it.

The key to creating a network is understanding the fact that most people, at their core, want to connect on a personal level, regardless of what business transaction is taking place. Whether you are looking to gain employment or are already in a career that deals with clients and/or suppliers, you will use networking skills throughout your lifetime.

When I look back at the first few years of my career, I was lucky to have managers who took me under their wings. Some taught me life-long lessons that propelled me to success, and some exhibited behavior that taught me *what not to do* in professional situations. Through both sets of circumstances, I learned the following networking tips.

When presented with a networking opportunity:

- **Give your elevator pitch.** A good professional tip is to condense your bio into a 30-second pitch (the time it would take to make someone's acquaintance in an elevator). Practice your pitch at home in solitude so that when someone asks, "So, what do you do?" you have a clear, concise response that leaves your conversation partner wanting to know more.

- **Listen**. You may think networking is about telling people all about you, your education or your business. After you give your elevator pitch, the rest of your time would be better spent by asking good questions that directly relate to the other person and their business. You will be perceived as thoughtful and conscientious which will keep you at the top of the person's mind. The more you engage the other person in a good, healthy conversation, the more opportunity you will have to make a connection.

- **Be a good mimic.** Need a strategy to kick off a good conversation? Speak the same language. As you echo back a similar tone of voice and key buzzwords that the other person is using, you start to speak in a way which he/she understands and puts the person at ease. You'll find that people will be more apt to open up and interact with you, creating a comfortable association.

- **Avoid your buddy.** While you may have friends or colleagues attending the same event, being joined at the hip to your wingman will ensure that you don't stand out as an individual. Ask your friends to make introductions to folks that you don't already know, but do not use your buddy as a crutch by sticking too close. Get up the courage to talk to complete strangers and make a personal goal of meeting a certain number of people at each event.

- **Limit yourself to a two drink maximum**. Meeting new people may tempt you to enjoy an adult beverage to calm your nerves and give you some liquid courage, but remember, it doesn't take much to ruin a first impression. Limiting yourself to two beverages over the course of an event is a good rule of thumb. The more you drink, the more likely you are to forget our tips about listening, being a good mimic and avoiding your wingman.

- **Link with LinkedIn**. More so than Facebook or Twitter, LinkedIn has the reputation of being a professional social media site. After meeting new people, search for their profiles and send a LinkedIn request. If you end up having a positive business-related experience with this person, leave a recommendation for the person. Most people will return the favor. Another benefit of LinkedIn is that you will be able to keep track of people throughout their careers and have access to their web of contacts should you need introductions to folks with multiple degrees of separation.

- **Be sincere**. When we talk about schmoozing it can have a negative connotation. Being successful at networking doesn't mean filling your smart phone with people whom you don't remember. The goal is to create memorable connections that can build into long-term relationships.

- **Be passionate**. You want to be viewed as a real person with a passion for life. If you reveal nuggets of who you are *outside of work*, it is more likely that those you are networking with will want to connect with you *inside of work*. Be yourself, be genuine and you will be memorable.

Now that you have these tips under your belt, be ready to use them at any time. There are everyday situations (on the train, at the gym, in your neighborhood.) where, if on your game, you can make important connections that will lead to future sales or job opportunities.

CHAPTER 23

Technology and Social Media in the Workplace

Technology and social media are everywhere. Savvy professionals know how to use these tools to enhance their careers. It's likely that you already have some sort of online presence, but it's important to monitor and build it in appropriate ways as your career progresses.

Keep in mind that your employer may have a social media policy in place. Some companies restrict or block access to sites like Facebook and Twitter, while others are more relaxed in their approaches to social media usage in the workplace. It is your responsibility to know your employer's policy and abide by it.

Now is a good time to again review what online information is out there about you. You are a reflection upon the company for which you work, so try to remove any subjective content that you find. You may also want to check your privacy settings on Facebook. Determine who can see you photos, your wall and your posts. Consider untagging yourself from any photos that don't project a professional image.

QUICK TIP: NEVER post anything online that could be construed as derogatory about a current employer or prospective employer. Many people have lost their jobs for posting inappropriate comments about the company, their manager or the projects on which they were working. Think before you post!

CHAPTER 24

Building a Personal Brand

Finding out information about other people is much easier than it used to be. Professionals are now going to great lengths to create their own personal brands online. For example, many people have purchased their own name as a domain and use the space for a portfolio, online résumé or personal blog. Domain names are relatively inexpensive and it might be worth the cost to show prospective employers what you have to offer. A personal website can expand upon what you fit into your résumé and may be particularly beneficial for people who are seeking jobs in design, art and technology fields to showcase their work.

Whether you decide to create your own website or not, make sure that your online presence is consistent. One of the best ways to do this is to search for your name online and see what results come up. If there are search results that are not appropriate for employers' eyes, take action to fix those items.

Be aware that anything you post online could be in the public domain. If you're posting comments or images online, they may be visible to prospective employers.

Online postings can be used for positive messages, too. For example, you can show your expertise in a certain area by posting comments on other people's blogs or creating your own. Consider subscribing to blogs and website feeds that offer tips for the industry in which you want to work and in your area of study. You're likely to learn something new and you may have an opportunity to engage with others in your field by posting comments and being a part of an online community.

If you don't have a LinkedIn account, sign up for the free version and post your résumé. Once you have an account, you'll have an opportunity to join groups of similar professionals. There may also be groups that cater to people who work for certain companies, people who attended your college, various areas of interest and more. The groups allow users to post their own questions, as well as respond to questions that others have posted. This is yet another way to become a part of an online community and network with people with whom you wouldn't ordinarily be in contact.

Once you have your offer letter in hand and all of the details of your employment have been confirmed, you should update your profile to reflect your new position. This information will show up in the status updates section of your fellow connections.

If you're concerned about how to build your network within LinkedIn, think about sending connection requests to current and former professors. It is also wise to connect with classmates and stay in touch with them as their careers (and yours) progresses. You never know when you might be in need of a contact at a particular company, a reference or a new job opportunity.

Google allows you to set up an alert that will email you any time your name shows up online. It's not fool-proof, but the free service does pick up the vast majority of instances that your name is in the media. If you have a common name, you may need to define your search criteria to include the city where you live.

CHAPTER 25

Cell Phones, Texting and Email

For many people, a cell phone has become an appendage of their hands. That's fine when you're enjoying free time, but constant usage of a cell phone in the workplace may not be acceptable. Check with your manager, or the employee handbook, to determine if it's alright to take personal calls during the work day. Some employers only allow personal calls in the case of an emergency.

Also note that texting and the use of abbreviations probably aren't the preferred communication method for interacting with your manager and co-workers. Email still prevails as the primary means of written communication in most companies.

Your emails should avoid abbreviations, such as LOL and ROFL. Spell out the full word and don't use "U" as a substitute for "you." There are certain rules that should apply when sending emails:

- **Be courteous** – your message should address people whom you don't know by their formal title. Use your manners by saying please and thank you when making a request.

- **Keep your emails short and to the point** – there is nothing worse than reading a lengthy email message that could have been summed up into two or three concise paragraphs or sentences.

- **Use a subject line** that concisely addresses the content of the email.

- **Grammar and punctuation count** – your message may be ignored if it contain typos and other errors.

- **Double check and proofread before hitting send** – reread your message to ensure that it makes sense and is free from error. Use spell check, but also proofread yourself because spell check doesn't catch every mistake.

- **Use reply to all sparingly.** This is a pet peeve of many professionals because reading a lot of irrelevant responses can be a huge time waster.

CONCLUSION

No one can give you all the answers to live a happy, successful life. There will be bumps and bruises along the way and there will be plenty of learning experiences, but try to make the best of those occurrences and learn from your mistakes to become an even better person and professional.

Just remember that you are not the first person to be experiencing the challenges of life after college and you certainly won't be the last. Learning new things doesn't stop after your last college class, so continue to hone your skills and do your best every day. You never know when that dream job will be offered to you.

Good luck!

ABOUT THE AUTHOR
Amanda Haddaway

Amanda Haddaway is a leader in the human resources field, as well as being an accomplished writer and marketing practitioner. She has been quoted in several national publications for her HR and marketing expertise.

Over the past decade, Amanda has worked in many facets of human resources and marketing, including recruiting, training, employee communication, corporate compliance, social media and advertising campaign development. She currently serves as the director of human resources and marketing for Folcomer Equipment Corporation, a multi-state construction equipment dealership. Prior to her employment at Folcomer Equipment, Amanda worked for SRA International, a Fortune 100 Best Company to Work For.

Amanda holds a master's degree from the George Washington University and a bachelor's degree from James Madison University.

For more information and to sign up for Amanda's blog, please visit *www.amandahaddaway.com.*

CONTRIBUTORS' BIOGRAPHIES

This book would not have been possible without the contributions from these experts.

Qiana Broughton is a wedding planner and bridal stylist at WeddingBlush, Weddings & Special Events (*www.weddingblush. com*). She lives in Northern Virginia with her husband, Aaron, and two sons.

Ed DeLise is the founder and President of Career Foresight, the leading edge software product that helps college students take ownership of their education and careers. A graduate of Texas A&M University, he spent over a decade helping the largest U.S. corporations understand their businesses better with Enterprise Performance Management software and consulting services. Helping students get excited about taking advantage of their opportunities to thrive is what drives Ed and Career Foresight to continue to find unique and powerful ways to make this a reality for as many students as possible. He is the proud father of 7, expecting #8 in November 2011. *www.careerforesight.com*

Constance Dunn, M.A., Presentation Specialist and Author. Yearning to look as polished as a classic glitter ball, Constance Dunn studied and innovated the ways to self-optimize in the areas of grooming, style and manner. As a researcher, writer and speaker, she instructs men and women how to architect their best look from a total 360° perspective, and enjoy all the benefits that come with it. Constance's book, *Practical Glamour* (RLD Publications, 2010), is a guide to finding and presenting your most authentic and attractive self to the world--no matter your age, budget or position. *www.constancedunn.com*

Kristy Jackson is a career counselor, employment consultant and writer with more than 10 years of experience in connecting young adults to the workplace. She has worked with students at both the high school and college levels, and has worked in management and human resources in a business setting. Currently, she serves as a consultant at the East Dakota Education Cooperative, where she assists area schools in developing more effective career development programming. Reach her at *kjackson@edec.org*.

Eileen Schlesier is a freelance writer, small business coach, wife to Kevin and mother to Natalie and Gus. A professional who values a work-life balance, she is passionate about coaching other female small business owners to self-employment success. To schedule a free small business consultation contact Eileen here: *www.sleeveshirtconsulting.com*.

Shannon Smedstad is a human resources professional with more than a decade of talent acquisition and college recruiting experience, and has specialized in HR social media since 2008. She spent several years working in Washington, D.C., and has experience as a headhunter, the career services manager at a nonprofit organization, and a recruiting and social media lead at GEICO. (She speaks for and is contributing on behalf of herself, not any company.) Ms. Smedstad graduated with a B.A. in Speech Communication from Shippensburg University and happily resides with her family in Eastern Pennsylvania. Feel free to connect via LinkedIn or Facebook.

REFERENCES

6. Managing employer expectations

*http://www.ceri.msu.edu/wp-content/uploads/2010/01/
CERIWhatemployerswantyoutoknowaboutwinninginyourjobsearch.
pdf*

12. Professionalism and maturity

*http://www.ceri.msu.edu/wp-content/uploads/2010/01/Its-the-
Basics-Really-Recruiting-Trends-Note-2010-2011.pdf*

16. Talking the talk – why communication skills matter

*http://www.ceri.msu.edu/wp-content/uploads/2010/01/
CERIWhatemployerswantyoutoknowaboutwinninginyourfirstjob.
pdf*

Ask the expert: A crash course in table manners and dining etiquette

Corr, John & Mitchell, Mary. The Complete Idiot's Guide to Etiquette. 2nd Ed. Indiana: Alpha Books, 2000.

Martin, Judith. Miss Manners' Guide to Excruciatingly Correct Behavior. New York: W. W. Norton & Co, 2005.

Von Drachenfels, Suzanne. The Art of the Table: A Complete Guide to Table Setting, Table Manners, and Tableware. New York: Simon & Schuster, 2000.

www.ingramcontent.com/pod-product-compliance
Lightning Source LLC
Chambersburg PA
CBHW071254170526
45165CB00003B/1342